"Continues . . . to teach us more
how we are part of that eternal story." —Jane Patete

LOVING
IN GOD'S
STORY OF
GRACE

Elizabeth Reynolds Turnage

LOVING IN
GOD'S
STORY OF
GRACE

LIVING STORY BOOKS

Learning God's Story of Grace
Living God's Story of Grace
Loving in God's Story of Grace

LOVING IN GOD'S STORY OF GRACE

Elizabeth Reynolds Turnage

P&R
PUBLISHING
P.O. BOX 817 • PHILLIPSBURG • NEW JERSEY 08865-0817

Unless otherwise indicated, Scripture quotations are from *ESV Bible* ® (*The Holy Bible, English Standard Version* ®). Copyright © 2001 by Crossway Bibles, a publishing ministry of Good News Publishers. Used by permission. All rights reserved.

Scripture quotations marked (NIV) are from the HOLY BIBLE, NEW INTERNATIONAL VERSION®. NIV®. Copyright © 1973, 1978, 1984 by International Bible Society. Used by permission of Zondervan Publishing House. All rights reserved.

Scripture quotations marked (NLT) are taken from the Holy Bible, New Living Translation, copyright © 1996, 2004, 2007 by Tyndale House Foundation. Used by permission of Tyndale House Publishers, Inc., Carol Stream, Illinois 60188. All rights reserved.

ISBN: 978-1-59638-847-5 (pbk)
ISBN: 978-1-59638-848-2 (ePub)
ISBN: 978-1-59638-849-9 (Mobi)

Printed in the United States of America

CONTENTS

ACKNOWLEDGMENTS

The main and minor characters in our stories put a face to the incomprehensible love of God. God has written powerful love letters to me through the kindnesses of family, friends, colleagues, teachers, preachers, doctors, physical therapists, readers, and sisters. My heartfelt thanks to you all.

I must thank by name the ones who love me day in and day out, whether I deserve it or not:

My beloved husband of thirty-one years, Kip. You image the steadfast, tender, and strong love of God to me.

And our four children, Robert, Mary Elizabeth, Jackie, and Kirby. You have shown me the steadfast love of God in the way you love me and love one another.

INTRODUCTION

Love.

Philosophers, poets, moviemakers, and ordinary people have searched to understand and explain love since the beginning of time. A Google search on "studies of love 2012" reveals that the contemporary world thinks of love almost exclusively in terms of romantic or sexual love, although some studies focus on the brain's response to a mother's love or supportive relationships. Following current evolutionary science, it is popular to talk about love as a "primitive human instinct." One MIT professor has determined that romantic love is best understood in the context of economic resources.

In the midst of such cultural conversation, we must ask, to quote Shakespeare out of context, is there an "ever-fixed mark" of love? Is it possible to understand love, and more importantly, is it possible to live love in a world seemingly desperate for it?

The apostle Paul says it is not only possible; it is essential. In 1 Corinthians 13, often called the "love chapter," Paul shows the Corinthians their lack of love by describing its true characteristics. Paul begins with the strong pronouncement, "If I . . . do not have love, I am nothing" (v. 2 NIV), and concludes with the confident declaration, "Now these three remain: faith, hope, and love. But the greatest of these is love" (v. 13, NIV). Sandwiched in between these two statements is a long definition of love in about fourteen parts, depending on how you count. Every time I hear this passage read at a wedding, I wonder if the couple truly believes they will love like this

(I know I did!). Personally, I fail the love test with the requirements of "patient and kind" (v. 4), and I'm guessing everyone would admit they sometimes "insist on [their] own way" (v. 5). And as nice as it sounds to say love "bears all things, believes all things, hopes all things, endures all things," (1 Cor. 13:7), who can really live this out?

There is only one who can and has: the subject of our study and the object of our worship–God. God can love like this, does love like this, and amazingly, empowers us by his grace to love like this. Indeed, without love we are *nothing*, but with God's love, as we shall see in this study, we become *something*.

GOD'S STORY OF GRACE

Over the course of the last two studies in the Living Story series, we have learned the deep implications of God's story of grace as outlined in four parts:

- **Creation:** Humans are created in dignity, in the image of God, with meaning and purpose.
- **Fall:** When Adam and Eve chose to disobey God, they brought sin into the world. After the fall, we were alienated from one another and from God. Without God's intervention, humans are condemned to live out a small story of self-seeking love.
- **Redemption:** Redeemed and restored through Jesus Christ our Savior, who lived, died, and was raised to new life, we become "new creations." In this story of restoration, we are being transformed into people of faith, hope, and love. Our greatest joy is to bring glory to God by living and loving in his story of grace.
- **Consummation:** We await the day when Christ will return and complete his kingdom work, removing all evil and

sin from his kingdom. At that time, a new chapter will begin of living with and loving God forever.

LOVING IN GOD'S STORY

In this study, we consider the ultimate joy of our lives in God's story of grace—to love as God loved us. John forcefully and succinctly summarizes love: "God is love" (1 John 4:8). Through the entire narrative of grace, the theme of God's love transforming his beloved prevails: "We love because he first loved us" (1 John 4:19).

In this final installment of the Living Story series, we will see how faith, hope, and love come together as the core elements in a life of worship.

- Faith means trusting in God for life and hope rather than other gods.
- Hope means believing that God is doing brand new things in the midst of wrecked shalom.[1]
- Love refers to the process of transformation that Jesus' love effects in us. We love as we live in and tell our redemption story to a broken world sorely in need of a life-transforming story, the good news of the gospel.

We will begin our study by searching the depths and heights of God's love. As we will see, God's love exceeds the deepest emotion described in any love song and defies any attempt at calculation by MIT researchers. It is everlasting, covenantal, self-sacrificial, pleasurable, and merciful, among many other things.

1. For newcomers to the Living Story series, *shalom* is most simply defined as "the way things ought to be." It refers to the state of wholeness and flourishing in which God created humans and the cosmos. Humans were made to worship and enjoy God, to give and receive in relationship, and to work and bring life for the sake of God's glory. The fall wrecked this shalom; all of creation awaits the day of restoration of lost shalom.

God's love, far from economical, does not conform to our limited human expectations. The story of grace tells us that God's holiness and wrath at unrighteousness and sin cannot be separated from his love. Indeed, it is right in the midst of his wrath at our unrighteousness that we see his incomprehensible mercy. Knowing that humans are helpless to help themselves, God sends his sinless Son, Jesus Christ, as the final sacrifice for our sins.

To understand how God's love dramatically changes people, we will look at stories from Scripture and from everyday life. We will hear of people who forgive more readily, share their stories for God's glory, and love neighbors, strangers, and even enemies. In the process, we will become love stories with skin on, moving into the world to bear witness to God's loving grace.

THE GUIDE

This Bible study aims to bring the transforming power of the gospel to bear on your life. As you interact with this material, I hope you will experience the freedom to live in God's story of grace with deeper faith, greater hope, and more passionate love. The format is designed to take you into the grand narrative of Scripture, your story, and others' stories by giving you opportunities to pray about and live what you are studying. The following sections will help you go deeper:

Engaging Scripture. Here you will focus on a passage or story from Scripture and answer questions for insight, reflection, and discussion. This draws us to worship God and follow Christ.

Theological Themes. This section discusses a theme that God consistently reveals through Scripture.

Entering Your Story. This section takes the passage and shifts the focus to what God is writing in your story. Here you will be given opportunities to write and tell your story.

Living Story. This section invites you to reflect on how you will live out the gospel in the topic being explored.

Praying Story. The final section offers an opportunity to write or say prayers regarding the story.

Here are a few suggestions to help you get the most out of the Bible study:

Just do it! Stoics like my pre-redeemed self embraced this Nike slogan long ago, and it didn't always lead to love. While I don't want you to fall into the trap of doing duty, I do hope you will engage the material. If the only thing you can do is read the Scripture, make sure you do that, because the Bible, the Living Word of God, unlike any self-help book, really does transform you! But please, do more.

Interact with the questions. The study is broken into five chunks of material to cover in a five-day period. This gives you two extra days! Use the space in the book, or, if you need more room, get a journal or create a file on your computer for walking through this guide. Let the questions wander around in your brain as you commute to work or clean the kitchen. And then write some things down. You may think you don't need to write anything down, but try it—new understanding grows as we write.

Pray. Ask the Holy Spirit, whom God has given as "The Helper" to come alongside you, to be your primary guide in the process of learning and living story. Specific exercises for prayer are provided in each chapter.

Tell and listen. Each individual reflects God's story of grace in a unique way. Gift others by sharing your responses and your story. If you tend to be more talkative, remember to leave opportunities for the quieter ones to speak. Always listen carefully to others.

Enjoy. We were made to worship, to give and receive delight in God's story of grace. My deepest hope is that you will enjoy being transformed by the gospel, the amazing true story in which we are called to live and love.

May God richly bless us all as we learn the narrative of life and love in Jesus Christ, which God is telling everywhere, all the time!

1

LOVE DEFINED: GOD IS LOVE

The All-Encompassing Love of God

KEY THEMES

- God's love is steadfast, covenantal, merciful, gracious, and sacrificial.

- Knowing God's sacrificial love in Christ transforms us into people who love.

DAY 1

The assignment was simple yet seemingly impossible to me: draw an aspect of God's character. (It might have felt easier if I could draw!) It was the first night of a course called Spirituality and the Arts, and we had ten minutes to complete the exercise, so I picked up my pencil and began sketching. What I attempted to draw was a small, faded brown 1989 Subaru with a female

The supreme expression of God's goodness is still, however, the amazing grace and inexpressible love that shows kindness by saving sinners who deserve only condemnation: saving them, moreover, at the tremendous cost of Christ's death on Calvary.

—J.I. Packer, *Concise Theology*

---

stick figure sliding down its hood. Large, strong, sinewy arms encircled the whole scene.

Earlier that day, during a pleasant morning jog on a nature trail that wound through a Seattle office park, I had been struck by that same brown Subaru. A truck-driver had waved me across the crosswalk, but neither he nor I saw the little vehicle moving in the lane next to him; nor could its driver see me. When I finally did see the car approaching, too late, watching in horror, even as my left side was falling on the hood, I remember two things—first, the sentence that played in slow motion through my mind: "So this is how I'm going to die." And then, sitting on my rear, cross-legged, just as I had landed on the asphalt, repeating to myself over and over, "I'm not dead. I'm not dead."

What I wanted to convey that night in class was the sovereign, ever-present, shielding, powerful love of God I now knew in a brand new way. The Bible asserts that *love* cannot be defined without God: "God is love" (1 John 4:8). Love is a fixed reality about the nature of God—and God is a fixed reality about the nature of love. The narrative of Scripture characterizes God's love as, among other things, steadfast, covenantal, merciful, gracious, sacrificial, and transformational. Love is God's prodigally generous, contra-conditional, eternal gift. And it is in this love alone that we as humans know love.

Engaging Scripture

The entire narrative of Scripture is built on the undergirding theme of God's extraordinary, redeeming, covenantal love. God

16

does many things: he creates, he rules, he disciplines, and in all of his activity, he never ceases to be loving. In this chapter we will focus on five major features of God's love. To do so, we will take a walk through many books of Scripture, for God's love is woven through it all. The books represent many genres, including history, law, poetry, prophecy, gospel, and epistle.

1. Read Exodus 34:5-7.

    a. What actions and characteristics describe aspects of God's love?

    b. Exodus 34:7 states that God will not leave the guilty unpunished, that he punishes sin to the third and fourth generation. How would you respond to the suggestion made by some that this punishment is "unfair"?

Hesed Love

2. The Hebrew word *hesed* (Ex. 34:6–7) is often translated as God's "unfailing" or "steadfast" love. (ESV, NRSV, NLT use *steadfast* and *unfailing*; NIV uses *love* alone.)

   a. Read Exodus 15:13 and Psalm 89:1–4. What does the Lord's steadfast love lead him to do?

   b. Read Psalm 136. How long does God's steadfast love last?

   c. How does God's *hesed* love differ from human love?

   d. How does steadfast, unfailing, promise-keeping love affect you? (What is your response to this kind of love?)

⚜ Choose a verse from any of the passages in this chapter to memorize. Write it here and tell why you chose it.

DAY 2

COVENANTAL LOVE

Closely associated with God's steadfast love is his covenantal love–his powerful and perfectly faithful commitment to protect his people. As we saw in *Living God's Story of Grace*, God made and kept a covenant with Abraham, telling him that he would be the father of a multitude of nations. Throughout Scripture, God makes covenants with his people, who often break them.

In Exodus and Deuteronomy, God restates his covenantal love to Israel.

1. Read Deuteronomy 7:6-11.

   a. What does this passage tell us about God's love for Israel?

The wrath of God and his love are not to be set over against one another. His wrath was the expression of his love, no less than his justice was. For love is not soft indulgence; nor is the wrath of God a display of temper.

—H. H. Rowley, *The Faith of Israel*

b. What does God promise to do for his people? What response is expected from them?

PARADOXICAL LOVE: MERCY AND WRATH

2. As we saw in *Learning God's Story of* Grace, God steadfastly holds up his end of the covenant, while the Israelites repeatedly rebel, forgetting his miracles and despising his provision. The only appropriate response of a holy creator God to rebellion is wrath—righteous anger against sin. The paradox of God's wrath is that it is actually a loving response to his people for two reasons: first, because evil and sin actually destroy our hearts, and second, because our iniquity keeps us separated from the only relationship that will truly satisfy—our relationship with our holy Creator.

3. Read Psalm 78:17-22.

a. What kindled God's wrath against his people?

b. Based on these verses, how would you respond to someone who said, "God is not loving. Even the Bible says he is wrathful and destroys his people."

4. Read Psalm 78:38. How does God himself deal with his wrath? What do you see about God's love here?

₲RACIOUS ḶOVE AND THE ℕEW COVENANT

The Israelites go their own way, worshiping false gods time and again, but God, because of his steadfast love, mercy, and grace, makes a way for relationship, atoning for their iniquity. (A quick definition of terms: To *atone* means to make up for by providing a sacrifice. *Iniquity* in the Bible points to the broader state of guilt borne by sinners. *Wickedness* and *evil* are also used to refer to iniquity.) Ultimately, God's love leads him to make the unimaginable sacrifice, giving Jesus his Son as the Messiah who would live a perfect life, die a saving death, and rise from the dead to restore God's kingdom of love. Though time and time again God's people rebel, remembering his own steadfast love, he makes provision for the covenant to be kept.

5. Read Jeremiah 31:1–2, 31–34.

    a. What aspects of God's love are mentioned in these verses?

    b. What does God's love for his people lead him to do?

● Review your memory verse by writing it here or sharing it with someone.

The new covenant will be kept fully by Jesus Christ the Savior. Its fulfillment shows God's gracious, atoning, and forgiving love. Grace has been explained by using the acronym G.R.A.C.E.: God's Riches at Christ's Expense. Let's consider the riches that God freely gives in Christ.

1. Read Ephesians 2:1–10.

   a. What was the spiritual condition of God's children before Christ died (vv. 1–3)?

   b. What aspects of God's love led him to send his perfect, sinless Son to die for rebellious children (vv. 4–10)?

   c. What effect does God's gracious gift of redemption in Christ have on our lives (vv. 5–7, 10)? How have you seen God's love change you or others?

2. Read 1 John 4:7–12.

   a. How does John explain his assertion that "God is love" (vv. 9–10)?

   b. According to John, how does God's love change us (vv. 7, 11–12)?

   c. What security, hope, or confidence do you receive from knowing the nature of God's love?

● Review your memory verse by posting it on social media or writing it in a note or an email.

Theological Theme: Atonement

Atonement is one of those theological words that is really much simpler than it sounds. It is made up of two basic words, with a suffix: "at" "one" "-ment." It refers to the "at-one-ness" between God and his people as a result of Christ's sacrifice.

According to the covenant of law that God made with Moses and the Israelites, God's people were required to keep the Ten Commandments. If they did not, they had to make "atonement"—a sacrifice for their sin—to restore relationship with God. There was a Day of Atonement (Lev. 16:34), when the priest sprinkled the blood of a sacrificial goat on the "atonement cover" in the Most Holy Place.

However, as Psalm 78:38 makes clear, this system of atonement would never be enough to make up for the Israelites' repeated and rampant sin. The fact is, we are born sinners, whose hearts rebel against God (Rom. 3:23). A permanent sacrifice for sins was necessary for unrighteous people to be united with a holy God (Ps. 5:4–6; Rom. 1:18). This is why God sent his Son into the world to live and die for us. In his holiness and justice, God removed his own wrath by offering the atoning sacrifice of Jesus Christ, his sinless Son (Rom. 3:25). In his death on the cross, Christ became our substitute and did for us what we were powerless to do ourselves—paid the debt for our sins (1 John 2:2; Heb. 9:28).

The result of the atonement is that we are reconciled to God, adopted as sons (1 John 3:1–2), created anew, and redeemed to bear Christ's love into the world (2 Cor. 5:17–21).

It is one of the New Testament's resounding paradoxes that it is God's love that averts God's wrath from us, and indeed that it is precisely in this averting of wrath that we see what real love is.

—Leon Morris, "1 John," *New Bible Commentary*

DAY 4

ENTERING YOUR STORY

God is love; God's love changes humans. One of my favorite stories is of Mincaye, the murderer turned missionary.

He did not know that his tribe was nicknamed, by some, the "Aucas," which meant "naked savage." He did know that all of his life he had been taught to distrust and hate anyone who might threaten him, his family, or his territory. So he plunged the spear deeper. Yes, these men had dropped gifts from the strange gigantic flying machine, and his tribe had enjoyed them. But that didn't mean the intruders were welcome in tribal land. Mincaye and the others killed the men to keep them from stealing their women and burning their homes.

So goes part one of the story of Mincaye, the young Waodani Indian of the Amazon tribe. The second part is far more astounding. Some sixty years after Mincaye killed the white invader, he travels the world as a missionary speaking about the God that white man came to tell him about. He does so with Steve Saint, the white man's son. A few years after five missionaries refused to defend their lives with the guns they had, two women visited the Waodani tribe to show them the love of Jesus. They lived among the tribe, healing and teaching, and telling about the God who made a way to end the violence. It was this love that drastically changed "violent savages" into a spiritually transformed people.[1]

1. The information on Mincaye and Steve Saint throughout this day comes from the following sources: Steven Curtis Chapman and Scotty Smith, *Restoring Broken Things: What Happens When We Catch a Vision of the New World Jesus Is Creating* (Nashville : Thomas Nelson, 2007); Michael O'Sullivan, "Friendship: An Incredible Act of Forgiveness," *Washington Post*, January 20, 2006, available online at http://www.washingtonpost.com /wp-dyn/content/article/2006/01/19/AR2006011901309.html; and Brian Mansfield, "Chapman Show's High Note Is Salute to Reconciliation," *USA Today*, April 18, 2002, available online at http://usatoday30.usatoday.com/life/music/2002/2002-04-18 -chapman.htm. To hear Mincaye tell this story yourself, visit http://www.youtube .com/watch?v=2JPkIJzIn7k.

As I hear Mincaye speak, I am struck by the reality that I too am a "violent savage." I have speared my husband with my biting sarcasm, my children with my hot temper, and strangers with my harsh judgment. And yet, because of how God's love is working in me, I can see the glimmers of a new compassion and mercy rising in my heart; I feel a stab in my own heart at thoughts, words, and deeds that harm a soul, and I turn quickly to confess my sins to the God who loves me unfailingly.

Choose one of the following topics to reflect on your story.

1. Tell about a time someone communicated God's steadfast, covenantal, gracious, merciful, or disciplining love in such a way that you understood it more deeply.

   a. Who was this person? What did they do to show this love?

   b. How did their love change you?

2. Steve Saint says that when his father was killed, his world was shattered, and he could see no way that God could bring good out of his loss. When Steve was eight, Mincaye, who had become a follower of Christ, asked Steve's mother who would teach her son all the skills he needed to survive in the Amazon (like making poisonous darts!). Steve's mother asked Mincaye who he thought should do it, and Mincaye offered himself. In a remarkable reversal, the man who killed Steve Saint's father became his substitute father.[2]

   a. Tell about how God redeemed a tragic story in a remarkable or unexpected way.

   b. What sacrifices were made, and who made them? What reconciliation or restoration resulted?

2. Discussed in Nell Minow, "Learning to Forgive," *Beliefnet*, accessed January 2, 2014, http://www.beliefnet.com/Entertainment/Movies/2006/01/Learning-To-Forgive.aspx#; and in O'Sullivan, "Friendship," *Washington Post*.

To come to see that God's love is a deep, warm love—a love constantly lavished on us quite irrespective of our merits, a love that cost the cross—is to reach a turning point. It is impossible to experience this love and remain unchanged.

—Leon Morris, *Testaments of Love*

⚘ Review your memory verse by writing it somewhere or saying it aloud. (If you have a smartphone, consider recording the verse and playing it back throughout the day.)

DAY 5

LIVING STORY

1. Begin to think about specific qualities of God's love that you would like to see grow in your life. Write some actions you could take that would demonstrate this characteristic. What power will you need to live this story?

   Example: I would like to be more merciful. This would mean being more patient and waiting for God to carry out justice, not taking matters into my own hands (or tongue!). I will need to keep my mouth closed, and I need the strong reminders of the Holy Spirit to overrule my tendency to make quick judgments.

PRAYING STORY

Write specific prayer requests for yourself and your group members, especially seeking God to change your heart by drawing you to love in new ways. Together, pray for one another, or pray the following prayer aloud.

Lord God,

Your compassion and mercy is bolstered by your steadfastness, discipline, and covenantal love. Your grace supplied the sacrifice for sin. Your tenacious love softened our hearts to receive the only love that will truly make us free. May we humbly and happily shout your love to the nations. Give us the words to speak and the lives to bear your how-can-it-be love into a world desperate to know it. May your name be glorified!

Moving Forward

With a deeper understanding of the wondrous love of our Maker and Redeemer, we are ready to explore further. In the next chapter, we will consider the nature of humanity and find ourselves completely undeserving of God's love. The reality is that without God's compassionate and faithful intervention, we are wandering, faithless lovers, seeking whatever god seems to satisfy at the moment.

2

IF GOD IS LOVE, WHO ARE WE?

The Loving God and His Adulterous People: Hosea

KEY THEMES

- The glory of God's compassionate, steadfast, contra-conditional love shines more brilliantly against the dark reality of our rebellious, wayward hearts. His love compels us to turn away from the weak and wearying false gods we have worshiped.

- Jesus, our Bridegroom, paid the dear price of his life to purchase us from the slavery of sin. By his faithful love, he has transformed his people into his glorious bride.

DAY 1

Coming off a devastating and destructive relationship, I was *not* looking for a knight in shining armor when I met mine.

Even so, there he was, in an 8 a.m. biology lab I didn't want to take, perched on a stool across from me, asking me about the book I was trying to read before class began. With his deeply tanned face, his tall, strong build, and his letter windbreaker on, there was no mistaking that he was a jock. When he told me he had read a book by the same author I was reading, in my mind I laughed, "You're a handsome Georgia jock—I seriously doubt you've read a book." And yet, as we conducted the lab that day, I felt myself falling for him. (This had nothing to do with the fact that he turned out to be quite adept at frog dissection!)

The struggle I faced as my now-husband and I started dating was a strong sense of shame left over from the previous broken relationship (more on that later). I felt utterly unworthy of the love of this smart, handsome, and deeply affectionate young man. Why would this well-known tennis player, whose last girlfriend was a beauty pageant winner, want to date someone like me? He was my prince, but I knew I was no princess. I wanted to hide, but I also wanted to be loved. With steadfast, almost stubborn pursuit, my now-husband convinced me that he really did want *me*, just the way I was, and eventually I began to trust this love and rest in it.

Thirty years later, despite the discovery that neither of us is a fairy-tale hero, my husband and I still think our love story is strange and wonderful. The Bible tells of a much stranger marriage, of a bizarre match literally made in heaven. According to this true story, "once upon a time," God created humans to enjoy wholehearted intimacy with him and one another. Despite experiencing the sweetest love ever known, these humans went their own way, believing there might be better ways to fulfill the desires of their hearts. In a bewildering twist, the Bible says that God moved right into the hiding places of their adulterous affairs and married them—to his perfectly sinless, sacrificially loving Son. And so Jesus became the heavenly Bridegroom who transformed his church into a loving and faithful bride. And that is the greatest love story ever told. In this chapter we study the book of Hosea, which dramatically portrays God's contra-conditional love for his people.

The more we immerse ourselves in the Story . . . the more we will find ourselves revealed not as hopeless romantics finally getting asked to the ball, but as irresponsible prostitutes becoming the beloved queen of the King of glory, Jesus.

—Scotty Smith, *The Reign of Grace*

ℰNGAGING SCRIPTURE: HOSEA

Genre. Hosea, written sometime between 722 and 653 B.C., is a book of prophecy. Prophets do focus to some extent on the future, but its primary emphasis is on calling God's people to return to the Lord.

Context. By the time of Hosea, Israel had split into two kingdoms—the northern, called *Israel,* and the southern, called *Judah.* Having experienced great prosperity, Israel had begun following foreign gods, specifically participating in Baal worship that involved, among other things, sleeping with prostitutes. Hosea urgently calls Israel to repent from such unfaithfulness. If they do not, God will allow Assyria to take power over God's people.

The book of Hosea is perhaps best known for its dramatic depiction of the biblical theme of God as Bridegroom and his people as bride. In the startling introduction, God orders Hosea, the author-prophet, to marry a "wife of whoredom" (Hos. 1:2). Through the dramatic story of Hosea's painful marriage to an unfaithful bride, God proclaims his steadfast compassion and pursuing love for his adulterous people.

1. Read Hosea 1:1-2. What reason does God give for telling Hosea to marry a "wife of whoredom" (v. 2)?

2. Read Hosea 1:3-9.

   a. Who is the father of Gomer's children (vv. 3, 7, 9)?

   b. What are the children's names (vv. 3, 6, 9)?

   c. Each of the children's names is related to an aspect of God's discipline. What do the names mean, and how do they tell us something about the consequences of Israel's sin?

Note on *Jezreel*, the first son's name: Jezreel was the place where King Ahab established Baal worship. It is used here to show that the LORD will defeat Baal worship in the place it originated.

3. As we saw in chapter 1, God's mercy paradoxically addresses his wrath. Notice the sharp turn that occurs between Hosea 1:9 and 1:10.

   a. Look up Genesis 22:17. How does Hosea 1:10 show us that God's covenantal love is still operating?

   b. What will happen to the children of Judah and Israel (v. 11)?

   c. Read Hosea 2:1. How does God's love cause him to address the consequences of Israel's sin?

⚘ Choose any verse from Hosea to memorize. Write it here and tell why you chose it.

DAY 2

In chapters 2 and 3 of Hosea, the story of harlotry unfolds. Because of his deep love for his wife, Hosea tells his children to "plead" with their mother to repent (Hos. 2:2). Chapter 2 is a love poem that reveals both Hosea's and the Lord's urgent desire for their respective brides to return and avoid the harsh consequences of their sin.

1. Read Hosea 2:1-13.

   a. What actions of Gomer's are described (vv. 2, 5, 8)? Why do you think the language is so graphic? What effect does it have on you?

b. What consequences will occur if Gomer and Israel do not leave their lovers (vv. 3-4, 6-7, 9-13)?

c. In what ways can you see God's love and mercy in these punishments?

2. Read Hosea 2:14-23.

a. What sudden change do these verses communicate?

b. How do these verses foretell God's plan to restore the covenant relationship the Israelites have broken?

c. What words are used to describe the price God will pay to buy his bride (vv. 19–20)?

3. Read chapter 3.

a. What does the Lord command Hosea to do (v. 1)? How do you think Hosea might feel about this command?

God does not accept me just as I am; He loves me despite how I am; He loves me just as Jesus is; He loves me enough to devote my life to renewing me in the image of Jesus. This love is much, much, much better than unconditional! Perhaps we could call it "contraconditional" love.

—David Powlison, *God's Love: Better Than Unconditional*

---

b. What reason does the Lord give for asking this of Hosea?

c. What hope for Israel is again stated (v. 5)?

● Review your memory verse by posting it on social media or writing it in a note to a friend.

DAY 3

The remainder of the book of Hosea details specific accu-
sations of Israel's unfaithfulness and repeats the warnings of
judgment to come. However, even in the midst of this strong
proclamation of Israel's promiscuity, the theme of God's covenantal love prevails.

1. Read the following verses. For each, write what it says
   about steadfast love.

   a. 4:1–2

   b. 6:6

   c. 10:12

   d. 11:1–4

2. The book of Hosea ends with yet one more plea for return and one more promise of hope. Read Hosea 14.

   a. What words are the Israelites instructed to say when they return to the Lord (vv. 2-3)?

   b. What promise of restoration does the Lord make (vv. 4-7)?

   c. Read Revelation 21:1-5. What examples of restored shalom (renewed harmony, healing, restoration of broken things) do you see in this scene?

Theological Theme: Covenant

A covenant is a formal legal agreement between two parties. In our culture, the best known is the "covenant of marriage." God has made covenants with humankind since the beginning of time. In *Living God's Story of Grace*, we studied the story of God's covenant with Abraham, in which God promised to make Abraham into a great nation. When God brought this nation, Israel, out of Egypt into the Promised Land, he gave them the covenant of law—the Ten Commandments (Ex. 20:1–17). According to this contract, God would protect and provide for his nation, and Israel would obey the Law out of gratitude for God's care.

As we have seen in Hosea, God's covenant can also be seen through the lens of marriage. The problem is, as Hosea highlights, God's people are promise-breakers, not promise-keepers. It is in this context that the covenantal love of God shines more brilliantly.

Throughout the history of the Old Testament, God's people rebel, but he refuses to cast them aside. In Jeremiah 31, he mercifully provides for a *new covenant*: "I will put my law within them, and I will write it on their hearts. And I will be their God, and they shall be my people" (Jer. 31:33). Christ came as the fulfillment of this new covenant. In addition to keeping the legal commands, he died, giving his blood as a sacrifice for our sins (Luke 22:20). Through Christ's covenant-keeping work on our behalf, our sins are forgiven and the Holy Spirit transforms us, giving us the desire to glorify God by loving him and loving others (Heb. 8:7–12). When Christ returns, God's covenantal faithfulness will perfect us as his glorified bride (Rev. 19:6–9), and we will be united with God forever in joyful, unbroken intimacy (Rev. 21:5).

❋ Review your memory verse by saying it aloud.

ENTERING YOUR STORY

The book of Hosea acts like an electric shock, jolting its readers into recognizing our desperate condition. It may be difficult to acknowledge that we are like Gomer in her "whoredom," but when we look at certain stories of our lives, it's hard to deny the similarities. Many years ago, in the season before I met my husband, I experienced the astounding love of God as he wooed me back from a wasteland of my own destruction.

In my senior year of high school, I gave my heart to a boy. Our hometowns were two hours apart; we had met at a competition for a full tuition scholarship. He won one of the available scholarships; I did not. I had always wanted to attend this university, and now, with my boyfriend going there, I was more determined than ever to go.

We dated long-distance for five months, writing long love letters and meeting for proms and graduations in our respective hometowns. I always felt that he was smarter and cooler than I was, and I worked feverishly to keep the gift of his approval. I knew that I was betraying my first love, Jesus, in my devotion to my boyfriend, but I couldn't risk losing him.

The next fall, when college began, the Lord rescued me from my devotion to a false god in one of those painful stories that seemed like anything but kindness at the time. Shortly after my father drove out of the dorm parking lot, I called my boyfriend. Our relationship had seemed awkward and distant during the summer. When I arrived at college, I discovered why: he was actually dating someone else—a girl from his high school who now lived on my hall. He mocked me because I didn't know we were free to date other people; he mocked me because I had not received the scholarship. Like the idols of Isaiah 44, mine had turned on me: formerly a source of sprinkled approval, my boyfriend now splattered me with the toxic rain of accusation and misery.

In the midst of the shame and pain I felt, I rediscovered the unfailing love of my compassionate God. The healing process took many long months, but God tenderly wooed me. While thinking about that season today still brings sadness at my self-deceived worship of a young man who cruelly abused my love, it also arouses profound gratitude for the unceasing, ever-merciful love of God.

1. Reread Hosea 2:14–20. Tell a story of giving yourself to gods that did not satisfy. How did God meet you in that story? What did you discover about God's love?

2. Covenantal love

   a. Tell a story of how you or someone you loved failed to keep a promise.

The surprising and oh-so-relieving gift of getting caught is that Love simply longs for our presence, when we are too weak and wounded to do anything else to make ourselves lovable.

—Sharon Hersh, *The Last Addiction*

b. Tell a story of how God or someone you loved has kept promises unfailingly.

c. What have you learned about love from these experiences?

❋ Review your memory verse by writing it here.

LIVING STORY

> And they have played the harlot, departing from their God. (Hos. 4:12 NASB)

As my story illustrates, we have many ways of leaving our faithful Bridegroom for lovers who seem to offer the satisfaction we crave. Look at the following list of false gods and add some of your own.

- ☐ Living for approval. Possible clues: your day is ruined if someone does not seem to like you or your idea. Your mood is affected by how many *likes, re-tweets* or *re-pins* you receive on social media.
- ☐ Playing savior. You take on other people's problems and feel responsible for them.
- ☐ Work and money. You define yourself by the type of job and the amount of money you make.
- ☐ Consumerism. You always want the newest clothing, technology–fill in the blank. Perhaps you take on debt to acquire goods.
- ☐ Addiction. You turn to alcohol, shopping, video games–fill in the blank–for a sense of temporary relief.
- ☐ Name some others that apply to you.

Now, for each of the idols you listed, pray and ponder about the following questions:

1. How did you begin to find relief, love, satisfaction in this idol? (What were or are the circumstances that led or lead you to this worship?) Example: In the absence of affection in the home, some teenagers turn to alcohol or drugs.
2. What do you receive from this idol? What does it cost?
3. What would you have to believe about God to turn away from this idol?

PRAYING STORY

Use the questions above to write a prayer of confession, repentance, and praise.

Though they grumbled and failed and begged God to leave, God continued to lead them, in mercy breaking each idol they would have settled
for, prying from their hands the things that blocked their view of the
promise God would not forget.

—Jill Carattini, "Unforgettable"

When you gather, write specific prayer requests for yourself
and your group members, especially seeking God to change
your heart by drawing you to love in new ways. Together, pray
for one another.

Moving Forward

In our study of the powerful and *true* love story of Hosea, we
have discovered the depths and lengths of God's compassionate
mercy for us. Now we will look to see how Jesus loved a woman
who needed much forgiveness and knew it.

3

FORGIVEN MUCH, WE LOVE MUCH

Jesus, Simon, and the Forgiven Woman: Luke 7

KEY THEMES

- As long as we think we can earn salvation by keeping the law, we will never understand our desperate need for a Savior.

- When we understand how much we've been forgiven, our gratitude to God will pour out in a love that scandalizes the world.

DAY 1

Throughout my freshman year of college, I continued to struggle from the sense of condemnation I had experienced both in the breakup with my boyfriend and in the ways I tried to numb the pain in the aftermath. That spring I was offered a

49

summer job at a Christian wilderness camp that had played a key role in my early spiritual growth. The couple who hired me had been the first to teach me that the good news of the gospel came to broken sinners like them—and me.

My job as kitchen coordinator was to assist highly civilized teenagers in the fine arts of baking bread in a wood-burning stove and roasting fresh-killed rabbit over a fire pit. Facing this challenge, we all learned humble reliance on the simple prayer for literal *daily bread* (novice campers had a way of killing yeast or over-stoking the fire and blackening the crust). In this wilderness sanctuary, God fed my hunger for restorative grace. He called me out of shame to rejoice in Jesus, the Savior who does not condemn but forgives. I began to enjoy a new freedom in Christ, and by the end of the summer I took some risks to move in new directions.

In this chapter we meet a woman who, powerfully transformed by Jesus' love, risked looking like a fool to show her love for him.

ENGAGING SCRIPTURE: LUKE

Background

Genre. Gospel. The gospel, from the Greek word *euangelion* meaning "good news," specifically refers to the story of salvation in Jesus Christ. Though each of the four gospels (Matthew, Mark, Luke, and John) is tailored to a different audience, they all record Jesus' life and words.

Context. Luke, the author, a Gentile in a largely Jewish culture, knew what it was like to be an outsider. His gospel offers a unique perspective on Jesus as the Lord of the disenfranchised, featuring stories of women, common laborers, Samaritans, and the poor. Luke shows how Jesus defies the convention of his day by loving "sinners and tax collectors."

Jesus Loves a Sinful Woman

Luke 7:36-50 tells a story contrasting those who don't know their need for Jesus' forgiveness with those who do. To understand the story better, you should know a little background about Ancient Near Eastern culture. A banquet like the one Simon threw could have the dual purpose of honoring a guest and flaunting wealth. According to the tradition of hospitality, the host was expected to provide certain services: washing feet (usually done by a household servant), anointing the head with oil, and offering a kiss of greeting. The banquet hall was often open to the air, and the public was invited to stand away from the table and listen to the guest's words of wisdom. As we walk through this story, consider these questions:

- In what ways am I similar to Simon?
- In what ways am I similar to the "sinful woman"?

1. Read Luke 7:36–38.

   a. What information are we given about the woman who worships Jesus? Why might you expect her to hide in shame (v. 36)?

   b. What physical acts of love does she perform (vv. 37-38)?

c. What do you think drives her to go so far outside of cultural expectations?

2. Read Luke 7:39.

   a. How does Simon, the host, respond to this scene?

   b. What does his response reveal about him? (What words describe his attitude?)

3. Read Luke 7:40.

   a. How does Jesus respond to Simon (v. 40)?

Jesus wants Simon to stop judging and start looking. . . . Simon sees a category; Jesus sees a changed person. Simon has a rigid view of people, one that places people in a category and keeps them there.

—Paul Miller, *Love Walked Among Us*

b. What is ironic about his response?

❋ Choose a verse to memorize from Luke 7:36–50. Write it here and tell why you chose it.

DAY 2

1. Read Luke 7:41–43.

    a. In Ancient Near Eastern culture, a person who could not pay a debt could be sold into slavery or imprisoned. How might the debtors of Jesus' parable feel when the moneylender comes to collect?

b. What freedom and hope do they gain when the moneylender cancels the debt?

c. Why do you think Jesus asks Simon the question he does (v. 42–43)?

2. Read Luke 7:44–46.

a. Jesus asks Simon to look at the woman. What do you think he wants Simon to see?

b. Jesus contrasts Simon with the sinful woman. Study these verses to find their different actions.

Simon did not give . . .   *The sinful woman did . . .*

v. 44:

v. 45:

v. 46:

3. Read Luke 7:47–48.

a. What emotions might Simon be feeling in this moment?

   b. What invitation does Jesus offer Simon?

4. Read Luke 7:49-50.

   a. On what basis is the sinful woman forgiven (v. 50)?

   b. How did receiving forgiveness transform her (v. 47)?

The beauty of this story turns on Jesus' gracious love of both the sinful woman and Simon. Here we see Jesus loving two different types of sinners—one committed to self-righteous legalism and the other who has turned from a life of liberalism. Simon's problem is that he thinks he knows everything about Jesus, but he doesn't. In his pride, he refuses to serve

I cannot hope to ever love someone unless I am committed to forgive him. I cannot hope to ever forgive him . . . unless I know the rich, incomprehensible joy of being forgiven.

—Dan Allender and Tremper Longman III, *Bold Love*

Jesus. The sinful woman has discovered and believed Jesus' astonishing love (we're never told what happened before this incident, but we know it affected her deeply!). Her faith has saved her (v. 50), and her sense of profound forgiveness leads her to love much. This story calls us each to ask, "In what do I trust for salvation?"

- ❀ Write your memory verse in a note to a friend or on social media.

Theological Theme: Grace

We use the words *grace* and *gracious* frequently in our world: "She walks with *grace*," "say *grace*," and "be *gracious*." In the Bible, though, *grace* carries deeper significance than mere eloquence or daily ritual. It primarily refers to God's favor given freely to us and working in our hearts by the action of the Holy Spirit. In Luke 1:28–31, Mary has found *favor* (grace) with God, and through the Holy Spirit, she conceives the Christ child. God's grace is on the child (Luke 2:40), and Jesus ultimately reigns on the throne of grace (Heb. 4:16).

As already established, Christ atoned for our sin when he died on the cross; Christ is God's gift of grace to sinners (Rom. 3:23–24). In Ephesians 2:5–8, Paul repeats the word *grace* three times to make it clear that salvation is the gracious gift of God, not the result of our works. The last two verses reveal the essence of grace: "For by grace you have been saved through faith. And this is not your own doing; it is the gift of God, not a result of works, so that no one may boast."

Eugene Peterson says that grace evokes a response of gratitude; it is this grateful response we observe in the sinful woman worshiping Jesus. When we know the gracious love of God, we respond with generous love for God and others (Phil. 1:7; 2 Cor. 8:1). Grace flows from God as a river of love and springs from our redeemed hearts toward God and others as a fountain of gratitude.

DAY 3

ᏁNTERING ᏥOUR STORY

Recently I read an article about a well-known Christian leader who had committed sexual transgressions and proceeded to lie about them when they were uncovered. The author of the article notes that the leader who sinned eventually confessed his guilt, repented of his sin, submitted to church discipline, and was reconciled to his wife. And yet, he continues to be condemned and shamed—by Christians.

I have heard more stories like this than I care to know. There seem to be at least three categories that describe the course of fallen leadership. In the first, the Christian leader does profound harm but is not held accountable, leaving the wounded with a heavy burden of confusion and betrayal. In the second, the leader refuses to acknowledge or confess sin when it is revealed, and the community suffers deep disillusionment and the anger of powerlessness. In the third, the leader repents and submits, beginning a process of change, but the Christian community refuses to reconcile with him, preferring to look (and hope!) for more failures rather than following Christ's example of forgiveness and restoration.

These stories of failed forgiveness reveal that every redeemed sinner struggles with forgiveness, betrayal, shame, and reconciliation. In the midst of our quandary, one thing is clear—only as we depend fully on the Holy Spirit's work in our heart will we forgive as Christ did and receive forgiveness as he desires.

1. What struggles with shame over sin have you experienced? Have you ever experienced condemnation from others over your sin? Tell that story. Imagine that you are the Luke 7 woman. Rewrite the story as if you were the woman, bowing at Jesus' feet. How do you picture Jesus responding to you?

(Continued on next page)

(Continued from previous page)

2. Do you have a story of judging another harshly, looking down on another sinner, forgetting how you yourself have sinned and been forgiven? What similarities do you see between yourself and that person? What differences? What might forgiveness and reconciliation look like in that story?

● Review your memory verse by saying it aloud.

DAY 4

LIVING STORY

In his grace and love, God gives us the Holy Spirit to help us understand forgiveness better. Pastor Scotty Smith, in his sermon "Forgiving Normal Sinners and Monsters," has provided an excellent tool for contemplating forgiveness. Read each of Scotty's points and ask the Holy Spirit to examine your heart and show you what you need to learn. Write a sentence or two about any point that applies to your story particularly.

Forgiveness *Is*

☐ one of the surest and most shocking characteristics of the kingdom Jesus has come to establish on earth.

☐ God's *outrageous* generosity to us manifest in his canceling the *entire* debt of our sin *and* enriching us with the mercy-grace treasures of the gospel.

☐ for us *freely* because Jesus willingly took our place as "the wicked servant," thus paying the enormous debt of our sin . . . not in prison, but on the cross.

☐ what the gospel increasingly produces in our hearts as we remember and relish how God has forgiven us from *his* heart.

In Christ's death, the final price of our rebellion was paid. It is a mystery of love, "God forsaking God," for the sake of sinners.

—Rose-Marie Miller, *Nothing Is Impossible with God:*
Reflections on Weakness, Faith, and Power

Forgiveness Is *Not*

☐ denial or glossing over wrongs, amnesia, or forgetting—the offense will still be part of your history, but it does not have to control your emotions and define your life.

☐ betraying the one who was harmed—as long as it does not minimize the offense.

☐ condoning or excusing something wrong or evil—it does not eliminate all the consequences of the hurt incurred.

☐ always about reconciliation—forgiveness is not the same thing as trust.

☐ avoidance; to have a forgiving heart is to long for, work for, and hope for justice and peace while revoking a desire for revenge.[1]

DAY 5

ᴄᴘRAYING STORY

Write a prayer about forgiveness. Here are some elements you may wish to include in your prayer:

⚙ Gratitude and praise to God for cancelling your debt and giving you the riches of his inheritance.

---

1. All the points in this list are from Scotty Smith, "Forgiving Normal Sinners and Monsters" (sermon, Christ Community Church, Franklin, TN, August 19, 2007). The notes are no longer available publicly, but audio from the sermon can be found online at http://www.mp3olimp.net/forgiving-normal-sinners-and-monsters/.

- Confession of any bitterness or resentment you have toward someone.
- Confession of an offense for which you need forgiveness.
- Request for the power of the Holy Spirit to forgive in your situation.
- Wisdom about what forgiveness is and is not in that situation.
- Thanksgiving and adoration that God has made us ministers of reconciliation.

When you gather, write specific prayer requests for yourself and your group members, especially seeking God to change your heart by drawing you to love in new ways. Together, pray for one another.

Moving Forward

Forgiveness transforms hearts and lives. Not only does it lead us to move toward Jesus in love, liberated from cultural convention, but it also frees us from shame. In the next chapter, we will read another story of a woman so transformed by Jesus' love that she can't wait to share her story with the people who shun her.

4

Freed from Shame: Glorifying God

Jesus and the Samaritan Woman: John 4

KEY THEMES

● Jesus' contra-conditional, gracious love transforms sinners by exposing our sin and bearing our shame.

● When we know the surprising love of God, we become worshipers who love outrageously by sharing the amazing story of grace with others.

DAY 1

She opened the door just a crack, evaluating the locker-lined hall. Only a few stragglers remained, and she could sneak past them. Thanks to the fact that Mr. McClendon never counted people tardy, she could avoid the dreadful morning hallway traffic when she endured the cold stares and silent sneers from the other kids.

Mindy tried to look normal, but she knew she wasn't. Everyone thought they knew her story—how a senior had gotten her pregnant when she was a freshman, and she had given the baby up for adoption. But of course they had no idea of her much deeper, darker secret. They didn't know about the late nights when Mindy's pimp called her and told her to meet him at the Blackriver Hotel. They didn't know that the senior who had gotten Mindy pregnant was involved with a ring of sex traffickers. They didn't know that no one knew and that she had no way out.

Five Weeks Later

There in the hotel, trying to scrub herself clean of the nasty, sweaty odor of three more men forced upon her, she noticed a number printed on the cellophane soap wrapper. The next day, during school lunch, she found a deserted place in the senior courtyard. She dialed, and a woman picked up after one ring. Mindy was astonished that this hotline volunteer seemed to know "her story" without knowing her at all. Intrigued, Mindy agreed to meet this woman at the mall food court later that afternoon. There, in the large open space saturated by the strange scent-fusion of Chinese food and chicken nuggets, she risked sharing a single page of her story of shame.

As you may have already realized, this painful narrative actually combines the stories of several women entrapped by sexual traffickers.[1] Their desperate situations are similar to that of the woman whose story we will study in this chapter. Like the Samaritan woman, they sought a love that would quench their hearts' craving. Like this woman, they experienced intense, isolating shame. Like her, they needed someone who would neither use nor shame them. The Samaritan woman met that rescuer, the only one who could save her from her sin and bring her out of hiding. In this story, we see how Jesus' gracious love works powerful

1. To read more about S.O.A.P. (Save Our Adolescents from Prostitution), visit http://www.traffickfree.com/S-O-A-P-.html.

transformation, freeing both sinners and shamed to tell their stories of rescue and redemption, naming God as their Savior.

ᴇNGAGING ꓢCRIPTURE: ᴊOHN 4:4–42

Background

Genre. John is, like Luke, a gospel, telling the good news of salvation in Jesus Christ.

Content. The apostle John wrote to tell people that Jesus is the Messiah and the Son of God. He wanted readers to fully understand Jesus' identity so that they would worship God in spirit and in truth.

Let's look at the intriguing story to see how Jesus' surprising, gracious love meets a woman's desperate thirst for love that will never end in shame.

1. Read John 4:6-9. Let's begin exploring this passage by considering a few story elements.

   a. Setting: Where does this story take place? When? What does the time and place reveal about the woman? About Jesus (vv. 6-7)?

I believe that the grace of God heals the shame I do not deserve, and the shame that I do.

—Lewis Smedes, *Shame and Grace*

b. Characters:

> **Jesus:** What is Jesus' current condition (v. 6)? How does he love the woman in a way that fits his condition (v. 7)? What can we learn about love from this incident?

> **The Samaritan woman:** In Jewish culture of this time, men rarely spoke to women and Jews hated Samaritans. Based on that reality and the woman's words, what can you guess about the Samaritan woman's life (vv. 6–9)?

2. Read John 4:10–15.

   a. What is the "living water" Jesus is referring to (vv. 10, 13–14)?

b. How does the Samaritan woman respond to his statement (vv. 11-12, 15)? Do you think she is spiritually thirsty at this point? Why or why not?

3. Read John 4:16-20.

a. Why do you think Jesus commands the woman to call her husband immediately after she asks for the living water (v. 16)?

b. In what way is his naming of her sin both gracious and surprising (vv. 17-18)?

c. What do you learn about the Samaritan woman by her responses to Jesus' question and statement about her (vv. 17, 19–20)?

🏵 Choose a verse from this passage to memorize. Write it here.

DAY 2

1. Read John 4:21-27. For the first time in this conversation, Jesus speaks more words than the woman.

   a. What truths does he reveal . . .

      about worship (vv. 21-24)?

      about himself (v. 26)?

   b. What is surprising about Jesus' revelation? How does this revelation show his love for the marginalized?

2. When the disciples return from their bread-seeking mission, they discover Jesus talking with the woman.

   a. What is their internal response (v. 31)?

   b. Why do you think they don't ask Jesus their questions?

3. Read John 4:28–30 and 39–41.

   a. How is the Samaritan woman both freed and transformed by Jesus' loving engagement?

b. What risk does she take in telling the Samaritans, "Come, see a man who told me everything I ever did" (v. 29 NIV)?

c. How does her sharing of her good news affect the other Samaritans?

4. What can we learn from this story about sharing the gospel in truth and love?

"Come, see a Man which told me all things that ever I did." That putting aside of all affectation; that genuine simplicity was part of her power. Never try to be otherwise than you are. If you have been a great sinner, be ashamed of it, but do not be ashamed of that love which saved you from it, so as to refuse to bear witness to its power!

—Charles Spurgeon, "The Samaritan Woman and Her Mission"

Jesus crossed cultural, racial, and personal boundaries to reach the Samaritan woman with his love. Radically changed, this woman, who had known many lovers, becomes a true lover—a lover of God. She loves because she knows that she is forgiven. Knowing that she is forgiven, she is freed from shame. Freed from shame, she forgoes any false pride she might have felt and moves into the lives of former enemies. In his profound grace, Jesus has healed the broken cistern of her heart and filled it with his living water. Now love no longer seeps out of the woman—it spills over in worship of the living God.

⚫ Share your memory verse by telling it to someone, writing it in a letter or email, or posting it on Facebook or Twitter.

DAY 3

Theological Theme: Obedience

"By this we know that we love the children of God, when we love God and obey his commandments" (1 John 5:2).

When we think of obedience as a way to earn salvation through good deeds, it becomes a harsh and impossible duty. A full understanding of obedience reveals it as a response to Jesus' love, fueled in us by the Holy Spirit. To live the call of 1 John 5:1–3, we must remember the back story. Because of the first Adam's disobedience, no person is capable of keeping God's commandments perfectly (Rom. 5:18).."All have sinned and fall short of the glory of God" (Rom. 3:23). The good news of the gospel is that Jesus, the "second Adam," perfectly obeyed God's law of love, and through him "the many will be made righteous" (Rom. 5:18).

Our obedience, empowered by the Holy Spirit, is the natural response to God's gracious gift of Jesus as Savior. Because God first loved us, we love God and love others in both our lives and our deeds (1 John 4:7–8). When Jesus offers the living water of his grace, the Samaritan woman acts with the obedience of faith and love, running eagerly and risking boldly to share her true story of the Savior who does not condemn. It is this kind of unashamed love that characterizes the obedience of a person transformed by Christ. It is this kind of love, freely given and fully shown, that characterizes one who worships in "spirit and truth" (John 4:24).

Acceptance-centered obedience comes from knowing we have already been accepted; it is not obeying to *be* accepted. . . . We obey because God loves us, not to get him to love us.

—Tim Keller, *1 John*

ENTERING YOUR STORY

When we know our stories of grace, including the shame of our sin and the forgiveness of Jesus, we too will move into strange worlds to risk loving and telling the good news to others.

Rosa sat by her mailbox, waiting for Julie's mom to pick her up. She knew her brothers and father were probably inside making fun of her for going to church, but she didn't care. She would briefly escape from the yelling that grew louder with every beer her father consumed. Soon, she would be in the bright, airy room, tucked in the cozy chairs next to Julie and the other girls. There would be happy noise until the youth pastor started to speak—high school boys playing ping-pong or foosball, girls laughing and chatting. Since Rosa hadn't grown up in church, she couldn't really understand much of what the youth pastor talked about, but she liked the music, and the songs were pretty to sing. Wednesday night youth group and Sunday morning church had become her "happy place."

Over the next year, Rosa began to make some crucial observations. She recognized that, despite what her father said, Christians weren't hypocritical fools. God wasn't harsh and angry; he had sent Jesus to rescue her. Boy did she need rescue. As she began to read the Bible her Sunday school teacher gave her and listen more carefully to the youth pastor, she noticed how kind Jesus was to women and children. She wished her mom, who had killed herself when Rosa was five, could have known this Jesus. Maybe things could have been different. Without realizing it, Rosa was beginning to love Jesus.

Two years later, Rosa had become a follower of Jesus, and she wanted desperately for her father and brothers to know the peace that she felt. Life had not gotten any easier—one of her brothers had graduated from high school and moved away, so her father spilt more of his anger on her, but there was hope in the midst of the struggle. Every time she tried to explain to her family the reason for her hope, they laughed. When she went to church, they called her names: "Little Miss Righteous." When she got angry and yelled at them, they said, "Some Christian you are!" Many times she cried and called them names in her mind, but she still wanted them to know the good news she had discovered. Her Christian friends and pastor became a second family to her, supporting her in her struggles and encouraging her to pray for her family and wait.

Twenty years later, Rosa has matured into a lovely and deeply faithful woman, a youth counselor who helps teens from troubled families. She now lives ten hours from her dad and brothers, but she visits three times a year and calls her dad once a week. Though her dad and brothers still aren't believers, Rosa knows that they have tasted the love of Jesus—through her own continued compassion and ongoing prayers.

1. How do you see Rosa's story as one of obedience that flows from a heart knowledge of God's glory and grace?

2. The Samaritan woman was shamed by the disciples and likely initially sneered at by her community as she said, "Come and see a man who showed me everything I ever did." Have you ever been shamed for telling a story about how Jesus worked in you? Have you ever been lovingly invited out of hiding as the Samaritan woman was? Tell a story about that.

3. Tell a story of discovering a new sense of freedom in Christ. What did you discover? How did you respond?

DAY 4

LIVING STORY

In this chapter, we learned that being set free by the love of Christ compels us to give glory to his name. What are some ways that you can live as a worshiper in spirit and in truth? Here are some ideas. Check the ones that you would like to do. Add your own.

☐ Tell someone you don't know well the story of how Christ changed you.
☐ Show others God's glory by serving them—raking a yard, making dinner, mentoring a child ... add your own.

☐ Worship in a tradition different from your own. Attend a church service with a friend to learn other expressions of worship.

ᴘRAYING STORY

Write specific prayer requests for yourself and your group members, especially asking God to help you receive his kindness in your shame and risk boldly for the sake of God's glory. Together, pray for one another, or pray the following prayer aloud:

God of glorious grace, we praise you and thank you and worship you for your inundating love. How glad we are that you do not condemn us to the dehydrating death brought on by drinking from sin-cracked wells. Instead, you pour over us and into us the sweet and eternal grace of your living water. We praise you for your mighty torrents of compassion and calming streams of mercy. We thank you that nothing can block the steady flow of your kindness. May your living water transform us into people who eagerly share the good news of your beloved Son, Jesus Christ. May we grow in the happy obedience that flows from your gracious love toward us.

Moving Forward

When we fall in love with grace, as the Samaritan woman did, we will love others from an obedient heart. In the next chapter, we will explore Jesus' call to go into the community to love neighbors *and* strangers.

5

FORGING NEW COMMUNITY: LOVING NEIGHBORS AND STRANGERS

Jesus and the Samaritan Neighbor: Luke 10

KEY THEMES

- When we are reconciled to God through the sacrifice of Jesus, we forge new community by loving neighbors, strangers, and enemies.

- Embodying the love of Christ may require us to give up comfort, preconceptions, money, or self-interest.

DAY 1

Every scene in Tom Hooper's 2012 movie production of *Les Misérables* is powerful, but as strange as it may sound, the most unforgettable to me takes place in the dark labyrinth of the Parisian sewer. The main character, Jean Valjean, has rescued his daughter's beloved, Marius, who has been badly wounded in battle. As enemy soldiers approach, Valjean, a man of super-human strength, escapes by dragging the unconscious Marius through the sewer gate. He then lifts Marius to his shoulders and sloshes through the dark and foul sea of sewage.

Watching Valjean's eyes and mouth traced in a bizarre mask of muck, I was struck by the immeasurable cost he pays for a man he barely knows. He literally plunges into the mire of human filth to save the man Marius; he also risks his own life and safety to do so. (I will leave that part of the story untold since it's something of a spoiler.) As hard as it is to watch this dramatic scene, it provides profound insight into what Christ did for us—he took on the sewage of our sin, wearing it him-self, as he delivered us not only to safety but to glory. When we fully know and submit to this sacrifice, we understand our calling to move into the world to embrace neighbors and strangers with a costly compassion that grows in us through the grace-work of God.

ENGAGING SCRIPTURE: LUKE

For genre and content, please see chapter 3.

In the parable of the Good Samaritan, Jesus turns a self-righteous lawyer's question on its head, calling us to quit won-dering who our neighbor is and get busy loving anyone who comes across our path.

Divine Gift-love—Love himself working in a man—is wholly disinterested and desires what is simply best for the beloved.

—C. S. Lewis, *The Four Loves*

1. Read Luke 10:25.

   a. What does the lawyer ask Jesus?

   b. What is his motive in asking this question?

2. Read Jesus' response in Luke 10:26.

   a. Why does he ask the lawyer what is written in the Law?

   b. Why do you think he asks, "How do you read it?"

3. Read verses 27–28. The lawyer states the correct answer, and Jesus responds, "Do this, and you will live." What do you think Jesus wants the lawyer to see?

⚘ Read all of Luke 10:25–39 and choose a verse to memorize. Write it here, and explain why you chose it.

We must be very careful readers to see the pitfalls of the lawyer's question. First, he asks what he must *do* to *inherit* eternal life. The lawyer totally misses the point of the gospel—eternal life, life in the kingdom of God, is the free gift of God. The lawyer cannot understand that it is impossible to earn eternal life by *doing*. Jesus wants the lawyer to search himself and consider fully the implications of both the question and the answer. As readers, we see that this story raises the most important question of our lives: "On what basis are we saved?" The answer is simple–by loving God fully. How can we possibly do that? Only through God's grace working in us.

DAY 2

1. Read Luke 10:29-31.

   a. Why does the lawyer ask, "Who is my neighbor?" What would be a better question?

   b. What reasons have you found to avoid loving someone?

    c. Enter the story and picture yourself walking down the Jericho road, discovering the man beaten by robbers. What does he look like? What is his condition? Do you want to stop?

2. Read Luke 10:31–32.

    a. What do the priest and Levite do when they see the half-dead man?

    b. Why do you think Jesus chose these particular individuals to play the role of those lacking mercy?

3. Read Luke 10:33–35.

    a. How does the Samaritan respond when he sees the man?

    b. List the verbs that describe what the Samaritan does in response.

    c. As the Samaritan cares for the man, what sacrifices does he make and what costs does he pay?

[Jesus] changes the question from "What status of people are worthy of my love?" to "How can I become the kind of person whose compassion disregards status?"

—John Piper, "Love Your Unborn Neighbor"

4. Read Luke 10:36–37.

   a. What final question does Jesus ask the lawyer, and how does the lawyer respond?

   b. What do you think Jesus wants him to see?

The fact is, as much as I want to scoff at the lawyer for being so brash and foolish in tangling with Jesus, I am too much like him. I often want clear directions for what I must *do* to earn my way into God's good graces. Or I don't really want to love my neighbor, so I come up with rationalizations to excuse myself. Yet, when I remember that Jesus himself is the real "Good Samaritan," and that I am like the man, half-dead, desperately needing compassion, healing, and mercy, my heart kindles anew with the love that grace works in me. We love because he first loved us; we can fulfill the law of love only through the power of the Holy Spirit working in us.

- Share your memory verse by writing it in a note or on social media.

DAY 3

Theological Theme: Hospitality

Hospitality is not just a Southern tradition of offering a cold glass of iced tea on a humid summer day. As we read God's story of grace, we see that hospitality to both those like us (our familiar neighbors) and those unlike us (aliens or strangers) is an essential aspect of loving God and neighbor.

In the Old Testament, as we saw in *Living God's Story of Grace*, three strangers came to visit Abraham and Sarah, and one of them was God himself. Abraham welcomed them openly and called for cows to be killed and food to be laid, and as the strangers feasted with him, he (and Sarah) listened and learned more about God's covenant. In Exodus 22:11, the Israelites were told not to mistreat an alien; the basis for this command is that the Israelites were themselves once aliens in Egypt. God's people were called to love God, neighbor, and stranger because God had shown them mercy.

In the New Testament, the themes of love, mercy, grace, and reconciliation continue to work themselves out in the practice of hospitality. Romans 5:10 stresses the reality that we were once enemies to God but have been reconciled to him. In a passage that, rightly or wrongly, has formed the basis of many mercy ministries, Jesus asserts that those who saw his need and responded will inherit the kingdom of God. He lists, among other things, how people have ministered to him by helping others who were hungry and thirsty, strangers, or prisoners (Matt. 25:31–46). "As you did it to one of the least of these my brothers, you did it to me" (v. 40).

Finally, in the letters of the New Testament, hospitality is often mentioned as a basic practice of Christians. Leaders in the church are to be hospitable (1 Tim. 3:2; Titus 1:8), brotherly love is demonstrated at least in part by practicing hospitality to one another (Acts 28:7; Rom. 12:13), and the Hebrew Christians are reminded that some have entertained angels unaware (think Abraham and Sarah!) when they have shown hospitality (Heb. 13:2).

ENTERING YOUR STORY

I didn't do it because I wanted to; I did it because it was a class assignment. In a seminary course called Essential Community, our professors wanted us to have the nitty-gritty experience of getting close to a "stranger," someone we wouldn't ordinarily sit near, talk to, or care for—actually, someone we might cross the street to avoid. It was a Saturday afternoon; our professors gave us ten dollars and sent us out in teams of two on the streets of a downtown Seattle neighborhood. We were to find a homeless person, of which there were many, and invite him or her to lunch with us.

My partner and I discovered a man sitting on a bench across from McDonald's. He was old and stooped, with frazzled gray hair flying out from a frayed cap and a wiry beard that would have made Santa proud if only it were cleaner. He looked angry and puzzled at our offer to buy him lunch and finally agreed to eat with us if one of us went to buy the food and brought it back to him. "I'll stay here," I volunteered, and thus began a painfully awkward ten minutes. Trying to get to know his story, I asked him about himself. He mumbled that he flew helicopters in Vietnam. He told me he had a brother in California, but they didn't get along. It was clear that his mind was very addled, to say the least, so I didn't really know whether to believe him, and since he didn't seem to want to talk, I sat there wondering how he had ended up on the streets if he had once been connected to a family and competent enough to pilot helicopters.

My partner returned with the food, and with grimy fingers poking through fingerless gloves, the homeless man grabbed at the burger. He wanted ketchup, and my partner opened some packets, which our strange "friend" squeezed all over the food. Ketchup dripped from his beard and smeared his long, yellowed thumbnail, and he didn't bother to wipe it off. I offered him a napkin, but he didn't even acknowledge it.

I don't think we loved a stranger that day, and for that matter, I don't think the old man cared much for us or for his lunch.

But something happened that day—we saw and smelled and touched a stranger, someone who seemed terribly unlike us. And in seeing the stranger, we saw ourselves and we saw Jesus. We were the old man—bearing the stale odor of sin, unkempt of soul, and numb of heart. And while we were in that state Jesus ministered to us, just as he ministered to the man. He bound up our wounds and fed us and clothed us and gave us drink. I learned a profound lesson that day—we can love neighbors and strangers only when we understand that we all have the same desperate need for a Savior.

1. Tell a story of moving out of your comfort zone to minister to a person in need. What moved you to do so (e.g., compassion, "class assignment," seeking someone's approval)? What specific sacrifices did you have to make to love this person? What was their response? What did you see about Christ? About yourself?

2. Tell a story of a time you were the "man lying beside the road," beaten and desperate. Did someone show you mercy? Were you surprised by the person or the circumstances? What did they do to show you love? What did you see about Jesus? How did you respond to their mercy?

DAY 5

LIVING STORY

Let's look at Matthew 25 to consider some of the ways we can practice hospitality with both neighbors and strangers. Read each possibility and write an example of how you or your group might live it—with one another and/or with strangers.

● "I was hungry and you gave me food" (Matt. 25:35).

● "I was thirsty and you gave me drink" (Matt. 25:35).

● "I was a stranger and you welcomed me" (Matt. 25:35).

But you could say that hospitality saved us. We were once strangers to God, but are now welcome (Eph. 2:12); enemies, but now friends (Rom. 5:10). The Lord's Supper reminds us that we are traitors not just forgiven of treason, but brought in for supper.

—John Starke, "When Hospitality and Hell-Fire Kiss"

❀ "I was naked and you clothed me" (Matt. 25:36).

❀ "I was sick and you visited me" (Matt. 25:36).

❀ "I was in prison and you came to me" (Matt. 25:36).

ᏢRAYING STORY

When you gather, write specific prayer requests for yourself and your group members, especially seeking God to change your heart by drawing you to love in new ways. You might pray this prayer together:

Dear God, our Father,

We come to you, confessing our desperate need for your mercy. You have sent us your very own Son, better than a "Good Samaritan"–a "Great Savior." He found us on the side of the road, beaten and bloodied by our own sin and the sins of others, robbed of our hope and faith, already dead in our flesh. You met us in that wilderness, anointing us with your living streams of mercy, and in your hospital of grace, you nurtured us and restored us as your new creation. Now, limping still, we ask for your power and strength to move into this hurting world with mercy and love. Give us your eyes to *see* with hearts of compassion and your faith to *respond* with hospitable hearts that reflect the depths of our gratitude for you. In the name of our loving and beloved Savior, Amen.

Moving Forward

In this chapter, the Holy Spirit opened our eyes to the kingdom significance of loving our neighbor, whether friend or stranger. Now we will turn to the most astonishing and seemingly impossible call of God's grace—to love our enemies!

6

Found by God: Loving as Ministers of Reconciliation

Jesus, the Lost Sons, and the Waiting Father: Luke 15

KEY THEMES

- ❀ Only in naming ourselves as enemies of God, lost in our own willful ways, do we embrace the extravagant mercy God has shown us.

- ❀ In Christ, we become ministers of reconciliation, celebrating his love as we seek to love enemies.

DAY 1

"I sinned with a high hand . . . and I made it my study to tempt and seduce others." What famous writer penned those words? You may know that it was John Newton, who wrote the

You have heard that it was said, "Love your neighbor and hate your enemy." But I tell you, love your enemies and pray for those who persecute you, that you may be children of your Father in heaven.

—Matthew 5:43–45 NIV

hymn "Amazing Grace." His life story explains his astonishment at grace. An arrogant young man, Newton rebelled against his father, deserted the British army, and worked as a laborer on a slaving ship. After being mistreated by a slaver in Africa, he boarded a vessel returning to England. When a terrifying storm threatened to destroy the ship, Newton recalled some Scripture his mother had taught him before she died. In this pivotal moment began his journey of "being found." He became an owner of slave ships, believing he could bring a Christian influence to the practice. Ultimately, Newton came to see the folly of his belief, and many years later, he joined William Wilberforce in working to abolish slavery in Britain. Newton wrote, "I hope it will always be a subject of humiliating reflection to me . . . that I was once an active instrument in a business at which my heart now shudders."[1]

In the context of this story, we see that Newton was clearly not exaggerating when he wrote the words "God saved a wretch like me" and "I once was lost, but now am found." Newton looked at a lifetime of "lostness" and saw God's pursuit and preservation throughout. As I read about Newton's life, I think he must have loved Luke 15, in which Jesus tells the three "lost" parables. Each describes God's joy over recovering something precious. The parable of the "Lost Son," often referred to as the "prodigal son," shows God's extravagant love for enemies and his joy over the reconciliation won by Jesus' death.

1. The John Newton quotes throughout this paragraph are from "John Newton," *Christianity Today*, ChristianHistory.net, posted August 8, 2008, http://www.christianitytoday .com/ch/13lchristians/pastorsandpreachers/newton.html.

CENGAGING SCRIPTURE: LUKE

For genre and content, please see chapter 3.

Study of the third "lost" parable in Luke 15 has too often focused only on the son who wasted his inheritance. As we engage this Scripture, let's look at the way God's unfailing love, mercy, kindness, compassion, and grace flow extravagantly toward two sons who have made themselves their father's enemy.

1. Read Luke 15:11-12.

   a. In Western contemporary culture, convention varies regarding asking for an early inheritance. In Jesus' day, Jewish law insisted that a son received his inheritance *only* when the father died. The ancient Middle Eastern culture would have been shocked at the younger son's request. Given this context, what has the father suffered for his son? What attitude might you expect the father to have toward his younger son?

   b. Considering these two verses carefully, what do you see about the elder son? What does he fail to do?

2. Read Luke 15:13-16.

   a. What does the younger son do with his inheritance?

   b. The word *prodigal* can refer to wasteful spending or squandering. How does the younger son deserve to be called a *prodigal*?

   c. In ancient Jewish culture, only a desperate person would be feeding pigs and "longing to be fed with the pods that the pigs ate" (v. 16). What kinds of desperate situations have driven you or others to run to God?

3. Read Luke 15:17–19.

   a. What motivates the son to return home?

   b. What does he plan to tell/ask his father? What does his rehearsed speech indicate about the type of reception he expects from his father?

⚜ Read all of Luke 15:11–32 and choose a verse to memorize. Write it here, and explain why you chose it.

DAY 2

Jesus instructs us to love our enemies, to bless those who persecute us. In Romans, the apostle Paul lists several aspects of loving enemies.

1. Read Romans 12:14-21. Study the following summary of Paul's instructions for loving enemies.

   ● Bless someone who persecutes you—do not curse them.
   ● Rejoice with those who rejoice; weep with those who weep.
   ● Lower yourself to associate with the lowly.
   ● Do not repay evil for evil, but honor what is honorable.
   ● Do whatever you can to live peaceably with everyone; recognize that some people will refuse to live in peace.
   ● Never avenge yourselves, but leave vengeance to the wrath of God.
   ● If your enemy is hungry, feed him—surprise him by doing kindness.
   ● Defeat evil with good.

As you read through the rest of the parable in Luke 15, remember these instructions and consider how the father shows love for his sons.

2. Read Luke 15:20. What happens as the son returns to the father? What verbs describe the father's actions toward his son?

In many cases, bold love will unnerve, offend, hurt, disturb, and compel the one who is loved to deal with the internal disease that is robbing him and others of joy.

—Dan Allender and Tremper Longman III, *Bold Love*

3. Read Luke 15:21-24. Dan Allender notes that one crucial aspect of loving an enemy is to offer him or her the "surprise" of the gospel.

   a. List the father's actions toward his son. What is so surprising about them?

   b. Why is the father so eager to celebrate? What do we learn about God's response to our repentance? About being reconciled with God?

Some have suggested that a better name for this parable would be the "waiting father," because the father in the story has clearly been watching and waiting for his son's return.

The father sees his son from afar. I wonder how many times he scoured the fields hoping to catch sight of a distant figure on the horizon, his son returning. When he spots the very son who dishonored him in the worst way possible, he does something no wealthy man of that culture would do—he lifts his long robe and runs. When the waiting father reaches his lost son, he embraces him and kisses him.

The prodigal tries to offer his apology and suggest a way to pay his debt, but his father just keeps on kissing him, refusing to listen. He calls for a feast to celebrate and showers riches on his son. This is why Pastor Tim Keller has suggested the story be called "The Prodigal God," because it reveals the unfathomable generosity of God toward sinners. Some, including the elder brother whom we'll discuss next, might say the father is squandering his wealth on someone completely undeserving.

❀ Review your memory verse by reading or saying it aloud.

DAY 3

1. Read Luke 15:25-28.

   a. Where has the elder brother been while the feast was beginning?

   b. How does he discover what is happening, and how does he respond?

c. How might you feel if you were in the elder brother's position?

2. Read Luke 15:28-31.

a. Note the similarities between the father's approach to the elder son and his approach to the younger. How does he feed the younger son what he badly needs?

b. Note the different responses of the two brothers. Why do you think the younger brother is able to celebrate with the father but the elder brother refuses? What prevents the father from "living peaceably" with his elder son?

Do I want to be like the father? Do I want to be not just the one who is being forgiven, but also the one who forgives; not just the one who is being welcomed home, but also the one who welcomes home; not just the one who receives compassion, but the one who offers it as well?

—Henri Nouwen, *The Return of the Prodigal Son*

3. Read Luke 15:1-2 and Luke 15:31.

   a. How are the elder brother and the Pharisees alike?

   b. How does Jesus show love to the Pharisees by telling this story?

Both sons reveal something about two ways our sin makes us enemies of God. The first way is that of the younger brother, the attitude of liberal rebellion that says, "I'll do whatever I want; I don't care what anyone thinks." The second, the way of the elder brother and the Pharisees, is the attitude of moral superiority that says, "I don't need a savior because *I* keep the law." The parable draws us to see a third way. Jesus is the one true Son of God the Father. He left "home" to take on the sins of the rebellious; he fully obeyed God's commands to show the self-righteous that they could never keep the law. The third way is to rest in the reconciliation with God that comes through Jesus. By doing so, we become true "sons" of the Father, able to love friends and, even more improbably, enemies.

◉ Share your memory verse by writing it in a note or on social media.

Theological Theme: Reconciliation

One of the most painful consequences of the fall is the broken relationship between God and humans. After Adam and Eve sin in the garden, they hide from God then blame and shame one another and God. Because God's holiness cannot coexist with man's sinfulness, they are sent away from the garden (Gen. 3:21–24). The theme of alienation continues throughout the Bible. The prophet Isaiah tells us that our iniquities have created a separation between us and God; Paul explains that we were alienated and hostile in mind toward God (Eph. 4:18; Col. 1:21), and that our hard hearts made us God's enemies (Rom. 5:10).

The astonishing news of the gospel is that because of his great mercy, God reached out to sinful humanity through Christ and reconciled us to himself. You can almost hear Paul's "can-you-believe-this" astonishment as he writes, "But God shows his love for us in that while we were still sinners, Christ died for us" (Rom. 5:8). We can now have unbroken relationship with God through Christ. And the call to love comes in this—God "committed to us the message of reconciliation" (2 Cor. 5:19 NIV)!

It is because of this reality that we reach out to others as reconcilers. We once were lost, but now we are found! We once were dead, but now we are alive! The Father has thrown a lavish welcome-home feast for us, and we want to share with those who refuse to eat! It is bewildering but true—we love our enemies because God first loved us as enemies.

DAY 4

ENTERING YOUR STORY

I always thought Renée was the coolest mom. She had four young children, and I had four young children. She seemed relaxed and happy, and more importantly, she had not only survived four young kids—they were all thriving! On several occasions, her youngest two children, sixteen-year-old twin daughters, drove a distance to babysit for us, and their joyous spirit deeply impressed me.

One dark night, though, Renée's story turned tragic; this story showed me how extraordinary she really is. Her dear friend arrived at her door in the dawning hours of the day with the worst news one could deliver: one of Renée's twin daughters had been killed by a drunk driver. Now it seemed Renée's life would be about loss, confusion, heartache, and the unending question: "WHY? WHY? WHY?" The ache deep in her gut resembled labor pain, but this groaning of her womb arose from death and did not end in life.

In the midst of the agonizing swirl, Renée knew one thing very clearly—she had to forgive. She knew that Jesus not only calls but empowers his followers to forgive enemies, and she began to pray about doing so. Seventeen months later, on the day her daughter's killer was sentenced to 22 years in prison, Renée looked him squarely in the eyes and spoke three profound words: "I forgive you."

About a year later, Renée began speaking to teenagers about the dangers of driving under the influence. Within months, she recognized that the students needed to hear the story of the driver, Eric, whose actions had killed her daughter, in order to fully understand the consequences. Eric spoke via video, remembering his foolishness; before the accident, it had occurred to him that he could be charged with DUI, but he had never considered the horrifying possibility that he could kill someone. The video made such an impact that Renée eventually asked permission for her daughter's killer

Through the gospel we are restored to a new partnership with the Father and the Son, by the Spirit, in the family business of reconciliation, living and serving with him forever and "making all things new."

—Jimmy Davis, *Cruciform: Living the Cross-Shaped Life*

---

to join her in person at events. And it became evident that something extraordinary was happening in Renée's heart.

As Renée began to work with Eric, her compassion grew. Her mother's heart thought about her oldest son, who was the same age as Eric, and she felt sad that Eric had squandered his life in one thoughtless decision. Without really knowing she was doing it, Renée began to dream of redemption for Eric. And then one day, she was standing before a judge, asking for his sentence to be reduced by half, from 22 to 11 years. In November 2012, Eric was released from prison, eleven years early. He was reconciled with his family, but the more extraordinary reconciliation had occurred over time—as Renée Napier and Eric Smallridge joined in an odd partnership created by our loving God.

Via email, Renée shared these thoughts about forgiveness and loving your enemy:

One more thought about the forgiveness process. It is amazing how God blesses us when we are obedient to Him. I am experiencing huge blessings everyday. I really understand why He commands us to forgive and to love our enemies. The Smallridge family is experiencing blessings, too. I thought I lost all my joy and would never experience it again. . . . I have found joy! God is faithful.[2]

---

2. For a beautiful musical telling of this story, listen to Matthew West's song "Forgiveness," available at http://www.godtube.com/watch/?v=WLPKY7NX. For more on Renee and Eric's story, please see The Meagan Napier Foundation at www.dui promise.com.

1. Tell a story of a time you were an enemy to someone and they loved you surprisingly. How had you harmed them? How did they bless you? What was surprising about the way they related to you?

2. Tell a story about reconciliation with someone who was your enemy. What happened in both you and your enemy for that reconciliation to take place?

DAY 5

LIVING STORY

The profound reality about being new creations in Christ is that we are designated ministers of reconciliation (2 Cor. 5:17-18). By the power of the Holy Spirit it is possible to love our enemies just as the prodigal father and a hurting mother did.

Think about an enemy in your life, or someone you just don't like very much. Note: it could be an entire group–a school, a group of people in your church, the government.

1. Do I long for this enemy to be restored to me?

2. Am I "prodigally" generous with forgiveness and grace toward this person or people?

3. What would a celebration of reconciliation look like?

4. Review the list in day 2, question 1, and write down
   some specific ways you might love a current enemy.

ᴄʀᴀʏɪɴɢ Sᴛᴏʀʏ

Looking at your thoughts from the "Living Story" section
above, write a prayer about loving an enemy. Try to pray as
specifically as possible for your enemy.

When you gather, write specific prayer requests for yourself and your group members, especially seeking God to change your heart by drawing you to love in new ways. Together, pray for one another.

Moving Forward

Can we truly be at the "end" of love? May it never be! We have traveled far and wide studying and discussing stories of God's faithful love, compassion, grace, mercy, and forgiveness. But as we share our own stories of how we have seen God's powerful love operating in our lives in seemingly impossible ways, our faith, hope, and love will deepen. Next we will plan and celebrate a feast of love.

7

Feasting on Love

Sharing Our Stories as a Gift of Worship

KEY THEMES

- As we share and hear stories of grace, our love for God and one another grows.

- We worship God as we gather to celebrate stories of God's unfathomable love for us.

DAY 1

In the Living Story series, we have fully explored the core calling of every human being—the worship of God. As we saw in part 1, *Learning God's Story of Grace*, we are drawn to worship when we know the depth of God's grace. In part 2, *Living God's Story of Grace*, we learned that faith and hope in God grow when we remember how God has redeemed brokenness. And now, as we complete our study of love, we understand that God's infinite

So now faith, hope, and love abide, these three; but the greatest of these is love.

—1 Cor. 13:13

and unfailing love radically transforms us into worshipers who love God and others with faith and hope.

As the waiting father knew, we must celebrate God's grace by feasting together. We have many reasons to rejoice and many riches to share. In these pages, we will make plans for a feast of love, in which we join together to worship the God whose love never fails.

STORY FEASTING

Perhaps many of you have already discovered the mysteries and joys of story feasting in the previous Living Story Bible studies. Here we reintroduce the topic for those who are new to the concept, but you veterans will find some fresh stories and thoughts here, so read on.

As we have said, sharing our stories is essential to growing in faith, hope, and love. As we hear the stories others tell of how God has worked redemption in their lives, we often remember marvelous deeds God has done in our own lives. Listening to others' stories helps us understand neighbors, strangers, and enemies and draws us to love them in new ways. And telling our stories can be a gracious gift to others.

The "story feast" concept is based on the significant theme of feasting that runs throughout the Bible. God called his people to gather at appointed times to remember how he had rescued and redeemed them. Everyone in the community participated in these feasts: the very young and the very old, respected leaders and marginalized aliens. Traditional foods were an essential part of the celebration; meat, bread, and wine were offered and enjoyed in thanksgiving to God.

In the Old Testament, the feast of Passover celebrated God's rescue of the Israelites from slavery in Egypt. In the New Testament, the Passover feast takes a strange turn when Christ says, "I tell you the truth, unless you eat the flesh of the Son of Man and drink his blood, you cannot have eternal life within you. But anyone who eats my flesh and drinks my blood has eternal life, and I will raise that person at the last day" (John 6:53-54 NLT). Today, the church remembers the ultimate rescue, Christ's, as we celebrate the sacrament of Holy Communion.

One way we can worship God is to offer our own stories to God and community, naming both the tragedy and redemption of our narratives. Sharing our stories and hearing others' stories strengthens our faith, increases our hope, and compels us to move into a hurting world with love. Story feasting deepens the bonds of community and undergirds the mission of love that marks us as Christians.

Let me give you a brief example of how that works with an illustration from a story told earlier.

Remember the story in chapter 5 about the assignment to buy lunch for a Seattle stranger? My dad, a former English professor and one of my best editors, read that story and observed that the man may have resisted our buying him lunch because it upset his sense of order. Perhaps, Dad suggested, the man depended on rituals and structure to bring some sense of control over the chaos of his past and present. When I heard my dad's observation, I saw even more similarities between the stranger and myself–I too depend on structure and order for a sense of shalom in my life. My Dad's editing led me to see that the homeless man and I share that need to know Jesus as the one who has come to bring peace for those who will rest in him.

As you prepare your story, write or tell your story, and hear other's responses, you will see God afresh. You have a week to prepare for your story feast. Walk through the preparatory questions and get ready for the most nutritious meal you've ever experienced!

DAY 2

FOOD FOR THE FEAST

Feasts involve special foods. It may be a favorite treat you enjoy from the grocery store (double chocolate fudge chunk ice cream, anyone?), or it could be your grandfather's special barbecued rib recipe.

1. What "ritual food" will you share at the feast? What significance does it have for you?

Ground Rules

All feasts are governed by convention. Rules for story feasts help to ensure a safe and welcoming environment. Consider these five guidelines:

Tell your story purposefully. The main purpose of this story feast is to glorify God. Recognize that all sorts of stories glorify God in many different ways. This core purpose, however, does not mean that our stories have to be overly spiritual!

2. Think of a story that you like to tell. How might it draw others to see the beauty, majesty, humor, holiness, strength, kindness, or any other characteristic of God?

Tell your story honestly. Telling a story honestly means being willing to examine our own hearts. We have to open our hearts to hear what God and others have to say to us through the telling of the story. Ask the Holy Spirit to reveal more about who God is, who others are, or who you are in the telling of the story.

Tell your story honorably. Avoid the temptation toward gossip, slander, or vengeance in your stories. But don't avoid telling the truth or pretend that something cruel did not hurt you. Here is an example: I want to honor my parents always, but the reality is that their decision to divorce caused deep pain in my life. As long as I tell how I felt and don't stray to the topic of their mistakes or sinfulness, I am honoring my story and them. I may also tell a story publicly differently than I would tell it to my spouse, a trusted friend, or a counselor.

3. Think of a story of being harmed by someone. How could you tell that story honorably?

Listen to stories with integrity. We should seriously attend to others' stories. We should be willing to engage and always honor the privacy of the storyteller.

4. Have you experienced being listened to with integrity? What did the listener do to make you feel honored?

> I love to tell the story of unseen things above,
> Of Jesus and His glory, of Jesus and His love.
> I love to tell the story because I know 'tis true.
> It satisfies my longings as nothing else can do.
>
> —Katherine Hankey, "I Love to Tell the Story"

Take part. No one is required to tell a story (though it will be fairly dull if no one does). You are welcome to come and listen without the intent of sharing a story. But keep an open heart, because people often remember their own stories when they hear the stories of others.

DAY 3

Prepare the Story

Write the story.

1. Reread the story questions in the "Entering Your Story" section of each chapter.

2. Reread the stories you have written to respond to those questions. Choose one that you would like to work on some more and to share with the group.

3. Write it out if you haven't already.

(Continued from previous page)

DAY 4

Reflect on the Story

Consider any or all of the following questions:

1. What does this story reveal about you or others? What does it reflect about your style of relating to others?

2. What does this story show about who God is and what he has done?

3. Is there anything about the events of the story that makes you question the goodness of the heart of God? If so, take those questions to him in prayer. Review Psalm 77 for an excellent example of a psalmist crying out to God in confusion over the events of his life and the resultant reaffirmation of his faith.

4. What does the story reveal about sin, grace, or redemption?

5. Take your story to his story–the Word of God. Is there a story in the Bible that reminds you of yours? A character? A psalm?

DAY 5

Edit the Story

1. After reflecting on the questions above, rewrite where necessary.

   a. Take out details that aren't essential to the key point of the story.

   b. Add in details that would make the story clearer.

Share the Story

2. Each group member will be allotted about ten minutes for telling his or her story and hearing the thoughts of others. You can read a story that you have written, or you can tell the story from memory or by using an outline.

   a. Would you like to read or tell your story?

   b. If you are going to read the story, remember to engage your audience. Look at them and read it to them, expecting them to respond.

   c. If you are going to tell the story, make sure that you have the key points outlined. You've got only ten minutes, so it's important to focus on the essentials. Practice telling the story beforehand to see how long it takes.

FINALLY, THE FEAST

Ideally, you should feast for about two and a half hours:

30 minutes: Feast and fellowship.

10 minutes: Leader introduces story theme and prays.

100 minutes (maximum): Story sharing. Ten minutes per person, so if your group is larger than ten people, divide into two smaller groups.

15 minutes: Close with a time of prayer for one another's stories.

*E*PILOGUE

The lives of men and women are indeed transformed by the good news of the gospel, as we have seen in the Living Story series. That good news does not end with our study, but continues for eternity. To finish in a way that helps you to live this story in the future, I encourage you to look back, to remember, to grieve, and to celebrate the contours of the terrain you have walked.

DAY 1

Go back through the study (or all three if you've completed them and are really ambitious!). Find your memory verses.

1. Write them all here or perhaps in a separate place (computer file, sheet of paper) where you can revisit them often.

Where the most eloquent exhortation fails, the simple story of an event succeeds; the lives of men are transformed by a piece of news.

—J. Gresham Machen, *Christianity and Liberalism*

2. Are any stories in your life related to the verses? Write at least the title of each story, or the whole story if you have time.

DAYS 2 & 3

Revise your story from the final story feast. Consider the process of telling the story.

1. What kinds of responses did the group give you about your story?

2. How did you feel as you told your story?

3. Did you notice anything new about your story through the telling or through a group member's response?

DAY 4

Write down any specific prayers that you will pray for other group members based on the stories you heard.

DAY 5

Finish the story. Write down some reflections on what you have learned over the course of this study and how it affects the way you live and love in God's story of grace.

Although we have come to the end of this Living Story Bible study series, we never come to the end of learning, living, and loving in God's story of grace. Throughout our lives, we are always students of the gospel, growing more and more like Christ every day. As we part, I urge you to stay close to a community who will remind you of the good news, encourage you to hope, and call you to love. I'd love to hear your stories, so please write to me at etstory@earthlink.net. For more encouragement on living the gospel story every day of your life, and for additional materials and helps, check out the Facebook page Living Story and my blog at www.elizabethturnage.com. You can also follow me on Twitter at @elizturnage. Thank you for joining me on this journey.

Elizabeth

WORKS CITED

Allender, Dan B., and Tremper Longman III. *Bold Love*. Colorado Springs: NavPress, 1997.

Calvin, John. *Hebrews and 1 & 2 Peter*. Calvin's New Testament Commentaries, vol. 12, Grand Rapids: Eerdmans, 1994.

Carattini, Jill. "Unforgettable." A Slice of Infinity (blog). *Ravi Zacharias International Ministries*. November 19, 2012. http://www.rzim.org/a-slice-of-infinity/unforgettable/.

Davis, Jimmy. *Cruciform: Living the Cross-Shaped Life*. Adelphi, MD: Cruciform Press, 2011.

DeYoung, Kevin. *The Good News We Almost Forgot: Discovering the Gospel in a 16th Century Catechism*. Chicago: Moody, 2010.

Hankey, Katherine. "I Love to Tell the Story." In *Amazing Grace: 366 Inspiring Hymn Stories for Daily Devotions*, by K. W. Osbeck, 299. Grand Rapids: Kregel, 1996.

Hersh, Sharon. *The Last Addiction: Own Your Desire, Live beyond Recovery, Find Lasting Freedom*. Colorado Springs: Waterbrook, 2008.

Keller, Tim. *1 John*. New York: Redeemer Press, 2007.

Lewis, C. S. *The Four Loves*. New York: Harcourt, Brace, 1960.

Machen, J. Gresham. *Christianity and Liberalism*. Grand Rapids: Eerdmans, 1946.

Miller, Paul. *Love Walked among Us: Learning to Love Like Jesus*. Colorado Springs: NavPress, 2001.

Miller, Rose-Marie. *Nothing Is Impossible with God: Reflections on Weakness, Faith, and Power*. Greensboro, NC: New Growth Press, 2012.

Morris, Leon. *1 John*. In *New Bible Commentary*, edited by R. T. France, J. A. Motyer, G. Wenham, and D. A. Carson. Downers Grove, IL: Intervarsity Press, 1994.

————. *Testaments of Love: A Study of Love in the Bible.* Grand Rapids: Eerdmans, 1981.

Newton, John. "Thoughts upon the African Slave Trade." In *Amazing Grace: The Story of America's Most Beloved Song,* by Steve Turner. New York: HarperCollins, 2002.

Nouwen, Henri. *The Return of the Prodigal Son: A Story of Homecoming.* New York: Doubleday, 1994.

Packer, J. I. *Concise Theology: A Guide to Historic Christian Beliefs.* Wheaton, IL: Tyndale, 1995.

Piper, John. "Love Your Unborn Neighbor." Sermon delivered January 22, 2006. Available online at http://www.desiringgod .org/resource-library/sermons/love-your-unborn-neighbor.

Powlison, David. *God's Love: Better than Unconditional.* Phillipsburg, NJ: P&R Publishing, 2001.

Rowley, H. H. *The Faith of Israel.* Augsburg, PA: Fortress, 1973.

Smedes, Lewis. *Shame and Grace: Healing the Shame We Don't Deserve.* San Francisco: HarperCollins, Zondervan, 1993.

Smith, Scotty. "Forgiving Normal Sinners and Monsters." Sermon delivered August 19, 2007. Available online at http://www .mp3olimp.com/forgiving-normal-sinners-and-monsters .html.

————. *The Reign of Grace: The Delights and Demands of God's Love.* West Monroe, LA: Howard, 2003.

Spurgeon, Charles. "The Samaritan Woman and Her Mission." *Spurgeon Gems.* September 10, 1882. Available online at http:// www.spurgeongems.org/vols28-30/chs1678.pdf.

Starke, John. "When Hospitality and Hell-Fire Kiss." *Gospel Coalition.* August 2, 2012. Available online at http://thegospel coalition.org/blogs/tgc/2012/08/02/when-hospitality -and-hell-fire-kiss/.

ALSO IN THE LIVING STORY SERIES

Learning God's Story of Grace is a meaningful, inviting, and encouraging study in which Elizabeth Turnage lays out God's grand story and helps you to see where your own story fits. Engaging questions allow you to apply not only the study, but the entire story itself, to your own life. Unique sections help you to engage Scripture and live out the gospel in your own story.

In *Living God's Story of Grace*, Turnage looks at the redemption stories in Scripture, helping you to reflect on the stories in your own life and surrender your trust back to the One to whom it belongs. Each chapter focuses on a Scripture passage and is broken into four main sections to aid your individual study and encourage rich group conversation.

"Elizabeth Turnage understands the power of story, the power of God and Scripture, the power of prayer, and the power of shared stories in community."

–**Daniel Taylor**, Professor Emeritus of English, Bethel University, St. Paul

MORE BIBLE STUDY RESOURCES
FROM P&R PUBLISHING

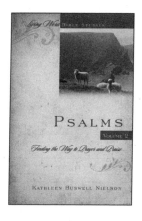

"Kathleen Nielson's inductive Bible studies have become standard tools for small groups reading the Bible together and eager to understand what it says and how to live it out. These studies do not replace commentaries; rather, by asking shrewd questions, they teach people how to read, especially how to read God's holy Word for themselves. This second volume on select Psalms maintains the high standards of the earlier studies."

—**D. A. Carson**, Research Professor of New Testament, Trinity Evangelical Divinity School, Deerfield, Illinois

ALSO IN THE LIVING WORD BIBLE STUDIES SERIES:

Joshua: All God's Good Promises • Nehemiah: Rebuilt and Rebuilding
Psalms, Volume 1: Songs Along the Way • Proverbs: The Ways of Wisdom
Ecclesiastes & Song of Songs: Wisdom's Searching and Finding
Isaiah: The Lord Saves • John: That You May Believe
Colossians & Philemon: Continue to Live in Him
1 & 2 Thessalonians: Living the Gospel to the End

MORE BIBLE STUDY RESOURCES FROM P&R PUBLISHING

The book of Revelation paints a breathtaking, majestic picture of our Lord and Savior Jesus Christ's coming again to complete God's plan of judgment and salvation. *Revelation: Let the One Who Is Thirsty Come* by Sarah Ivill is an annotated, expository Bible study that provides Old Testament backgrounds, commentary, and personal exhortations—distinguishing it from other Bible study guides.

"Sarah Ivill is a faithful guide."
—**Charles Dunahoo**, Coordinator of Christian Education and Publications for the PCA

From the private sorrows of Hannah to the action-packed reign of King David, the narratives of 1 and 2 Samuel make for a gripping read. But how do you best *study* these stories? What bearing do they have on Christ, the New Testament, or your life today? Kay Gabrysch answers these questions while helping us develop a lasting framework for reading biblical narratives.

"Gracious and accessible."
—**Michael D. Williams**, Professor of Systematic Theology, Covenant Seminary, St. Louis

MORE BIBLE STUDY RESOURCES FROM P&R PUBLISHING

This yearlong study of God's Word guides you through five acts of his grand story of redemption. Although you won't read *every* chapter in the Bible, daily Scripture and devotional readings will equip you to understand the unity and development of God's story and to grow in your personal discipline of Bible study and prayer.

"*The Story* provides concise, clear, brief readings that will help anyone and everyone deepen their understanding of the big story of the Bible."
—**Nancy Guthrie**, Author, *The One Year Book of Discovering Jesus in the Old Testament*

"An incredible resource for students to thoughtfully read the Bible. It's true to Scripture, engaging, and concise yet thorough."
—**Gloria Furman**, Author, *Glimpses of Grace*

Barbara Duguid turns to the writings of John Newton to teach us God's purpose for our failure and guilt—and to help us adjust our expectations of ourselves. Her empathetic, honest approach, candidly incorporating illustrations from her own struggles, lifts our focus from our own performance back to the God who is bigger than our failures—and who uses them for his glory. Rediscover how God's extravagant grace makes the gospel once again feel like the good news it truly is!

"I cannot commend this book enough. We need more and more books like this that remind us that the focus of the Christian faith is not the life of the Christian, but Christ."
　　　　—Tullian Tchividjian, Author of *Jesus + Nothing = Everything*

While striving to find meaning amid the mundane and ordinary, many women find themselves swallowed up by culture's expectations, trying to escape the labels that trap and define them. But Aimee Byrd is determined to reclaim terms like *housewife*, which have divided many women, to unite them instead in their common calling.

What is this calling, and how can women rise above what the world offers? By taking back another term—*theologian*—and knowing God intimately. Aimee will help you evaluate your Christian life and see your world from a different perspective.

"This is a fine book, written with gusto and infectious enthusiasm."
—**Carl R. Trueman**, Professor of Church History,
Westminster Theological Seminary, Philadelphia